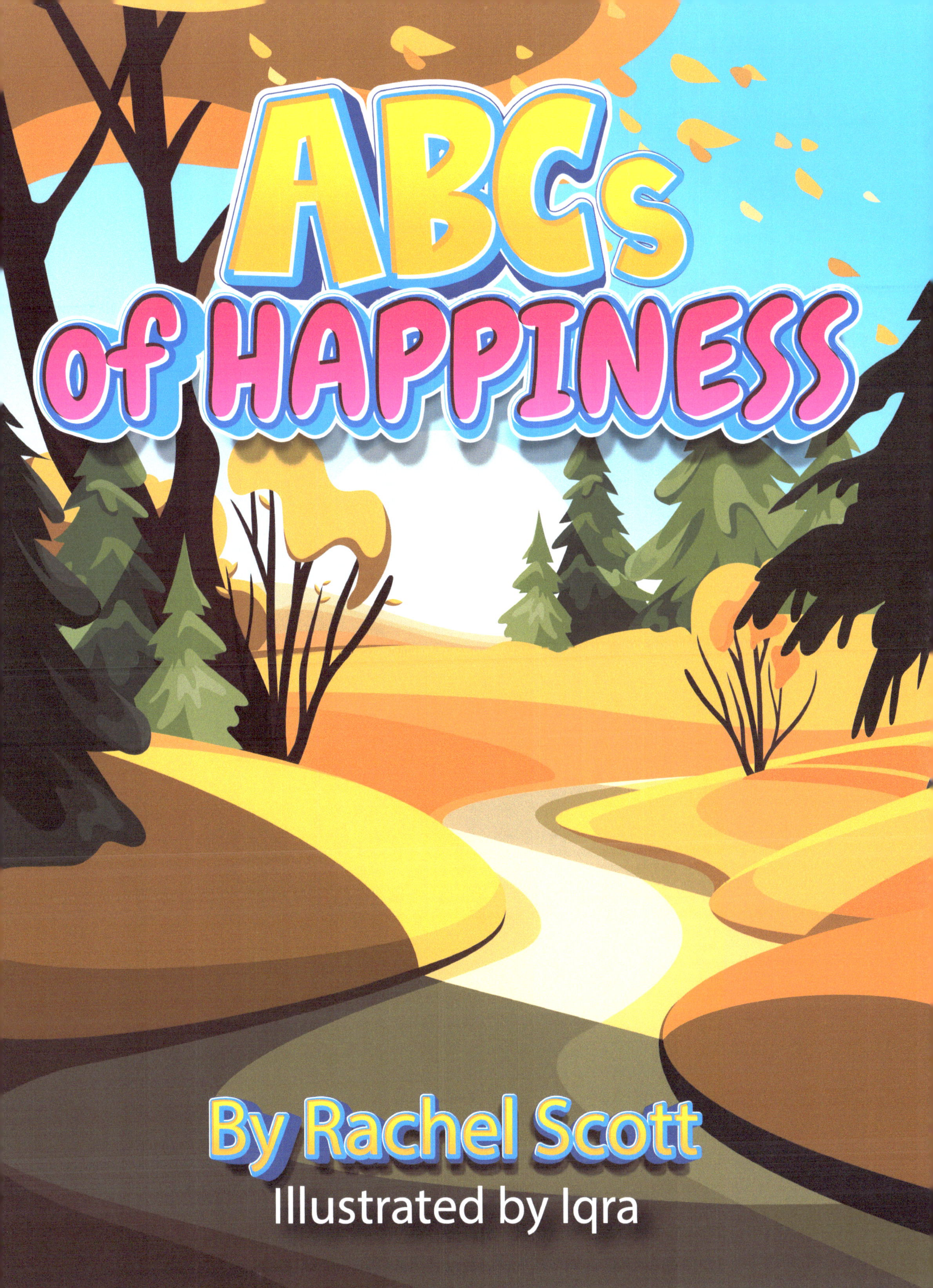

ABCs
of HAPPINESS
By Rachel Scott
Illustrated by Iqra

Dedicated to Ollie and Luca.
I can't wait to see what you
do on the zigzagging
road of life.

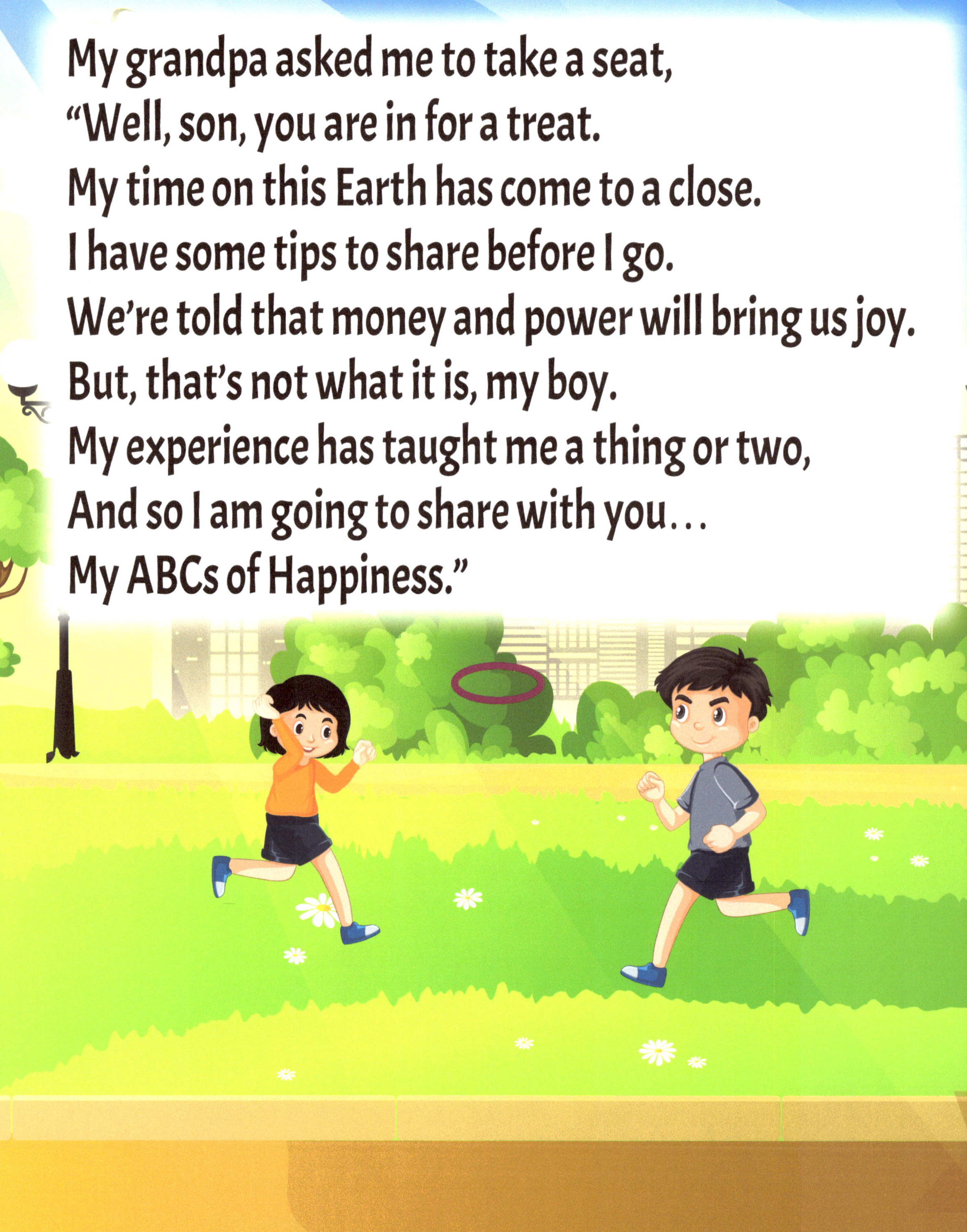

My grandpa asked me to take a seat,
"Well, son, you are in for a treat.
My time on this Earth has come to a close.
I have some tips to share before I go.
We're told that money and power will bring us joy.
But, that's not what it is, my boy.
My experience has taught me a thing or two,
And so I am going to share with you…
My ABCs of Happiness."

A is for **Affirmations** that keep your confidence high.
B is for **Believing** you will accomplish what you try.

"I will accomplish what I try."

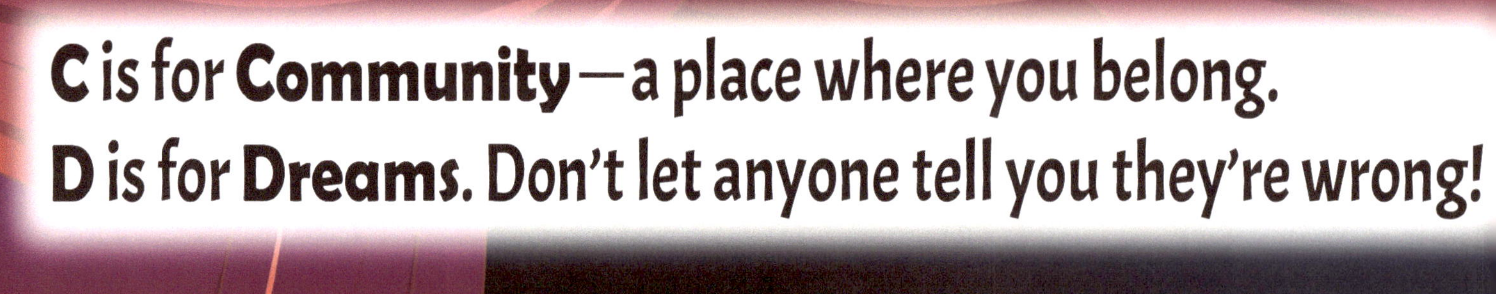

C is for **Community**—a place where you belong.
D is for **Dreams**. Don't let anyone tell you they're wrong!

E is for **Exercise**—whether you like to run, jump or crawl.
F is for **Family** who will support you through it all.

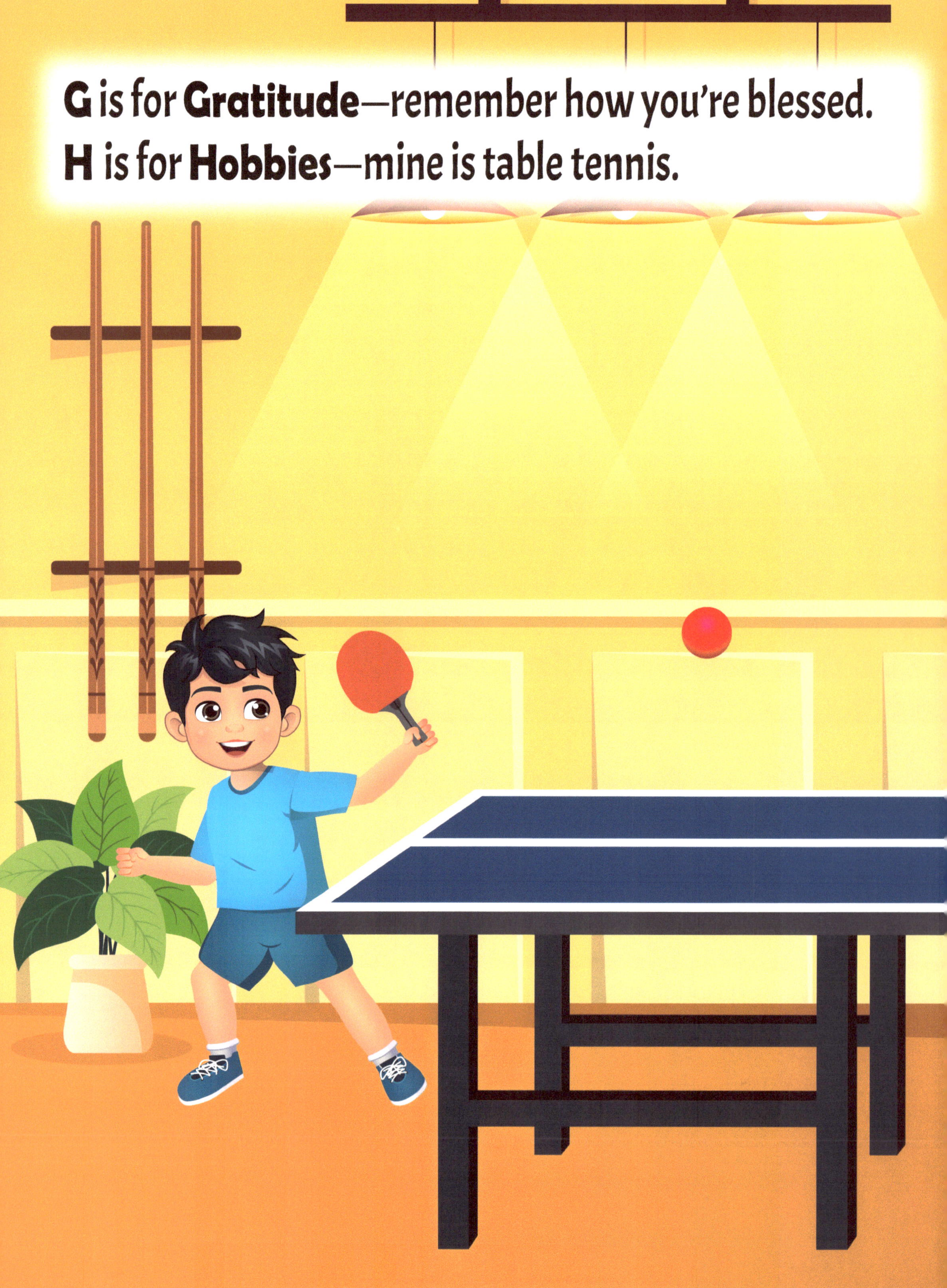

G is for **Gratitude**—remember how you're blessed.
H is for **Hobbies**—mine is table tennis.

I is for **Imagination**—transport yourself to a new place.
J is for **Journaling**—in a cozy, comfy space.

K is for **Kindness** that can brighten someone's week.
L is for **Listening** as much as you want to speak.

M is for Music—dance, play, listen and sing.
N is for Novelty—it's good to try a new thing.

O is for Outdoors—touch the grass and feel the sun.
P is for Play. What is life without some fun?

Q is for **Quiet times** that can bring peace of mind.
R is for **Reading**—some entertainment is offline.

S is for **Sleeping**—an essential key to well-being.
T is for **Traveling**. Enjoy new food and sightseeing.

U is for **Unwinding** with a friend or with a wife.
V is for **Variety**—they say it's the spice of life.

W is for **Walks**—they help to relieve the pressure.
X is for **X's** and **O's**. Write letters for those you treasure.

Y is for **Yummies**. My favorite is cheesy bread.
Z is for **Zigzag**. Embrace the winding road ahead.